Contents

Early Encounters

Reports of UFOs shocked the world. Some were sightings, but other encounters were more frightening.

On the night of September 19, 1961, Barney and Betty Hill were heading for their home in New Hampshire on U.S. Route 3. Suddenly they saw a bright light in the sky. They stopped the car. Then the light came closer. Barney had his binoculars in the car. Betty looked through them and saw a huge craft. It was a UFO.

Barney got out of the car and walked toward the light. It now appeared to be level with the tops of the trees. Soon Barney was close to it. It looked "like a big pancake," he said later.

LOST TIME

Barney and Betty were frightened, and drove away. Then, they heard "beeping" sounds that seemed to come from the trunk. The Hills finally reached home. It was dawn. They had taken seven hours to travel the last 190 miles (304 km) of their journey—at least two hours longer than usual for such a distance.

Soon Betty began to have nightmares. Barney could hardly sleep at all. In 1962, he began seeing a psychiatrist. After a year, he asked to be given hypnosis. He needed to know what had happened that night, two years earlier.

While driving home from a vacation in Canada in 1961, Betty and Barney Hill saw a huge UFO hovering above the treetops (opposite).

4

"Suddenly they saw a bright light in the sky. They stopped the car. Then, the light came closer."

CONTACT WITH ALIENS

Barney's hypnosis sessions with Dr. Benjamin Simon of Boston began in December 1963. Soon Betty joined him. According to Dr. Simon, both the Hills told nearly the same story.

Barney described how he had gone up a ramp to the UFO. Then he was led into a room.

"I could feel them examining me with their hands. They looked at my back. I could feel them touching my skin. It was like they were counting my spinal column. My mouth was opened. I could feel two fingers pulling it back. Then I heard as if some more men came in. I could feel them rustling around.

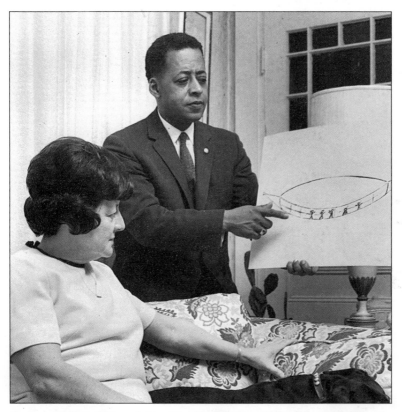

Barney and Betty Hill, social workers living in New Hampshire, describing the size and appearance of the UFO that abducted them in September 1961.

An artist's idea of what the aliens who abducted Barney and Betty Hill looked like. The drawing is based on descriptions given by the Hills while they were under hypnosis.

They were on the left side of the table I was lying on. Something scratched very lightly, like a stick, against my left arm. And then these men left. . . . I went down the ramp and opened my eyes, . . . I saw my car."

Betty's story was similar. She said she thought the aliens were taking samples for scientific study. One of the aliens spoke English. She asked him where the spacecraft had come from. He showed her a star map. Then Betty was led down the ramp to the car.

A POWERFUL FANTASY

After the hypnosis sessions, Betty made a drawing. It was a copy of the star map. Years later an astronomer named Marjorie Fish studied the case. She tried to match the map with known stars. She used a *Catalogue of Nearby Stars*, which was published in 1969. She made an interesting discovery about the map—it was like a view of the Sun and other stars. But the view was from somewhere beyond the star system known as Zeta Reticuli.

Other astronomers agreed that this was strange. Some of these stars were not known publicly until the *Catalogue of Nearby Stars* was published in 1969. And that was six years after Betty Hill drew her map.

Barney Hill died in 1969, at the age of 46. Later, Betty reported many other sightings of UFOs and told of having more encounters with aliens. However, Dr. Simon came to another conclusion. He said the Hills's stories were pure fantasy.

"The light came down. He could see a spacecraft shaped like an egg."

UFO SIGHTING BY ANTONIO VILLAS BOAS

The story of Barney and Betty Hill was not the first account of an alien abduction. Nor was it the last. One of the earliest reports was made by a Brazilian. His name was Antonio Villas Boas. He described himself as a farmer. On the night of October 15–16, 1957, he was working in his fields. He saw "a large red star" approaching.

The light came down. He could see a spacecraft shaped like an egg. It landed no more than 50 feet (15 m) away. There were purple lights along its edge, and it sat on three "legs."

A NIGHT VISIT

The motor of Antonio's tractor stopped suddenly. It would not start again. Antonio was alarmed and tried to run away, but he was caught by three creatures. They had come out of the UFO. They were about 5 feet 6 inches (1.65 m) tall and wore tight-fitting suits and large helmets. Antonio was taken aboard the craft. The aliens, he said, tried to communicate with him. But they spoke in "slow barks and yelps. These sounds were neither very clear nor very hoarse. Some were longer, some were short. At times they made several different sounds at once."

VISION OF BEAUTY

After a while, Antonio was left on his own. Then, 30 minutes later, the door was opened by a woman. Antonio described her as being "more beautiful than any I have ever seen before." They spent some time together. She seemed particularly interested in the structure of the human body. Before she left, she pointed upward at the sky. Antonio guessed she meant she would be returning to her home planet.

When the woman left, Antonio was returned to his field. The alien craft took off, "like a bullet." Mysteriously, four hours had passed.

Years later it was revealed that Antonio Boas was not a farmer at all. In fact, he was a lawyer. People began to doubt his story. He had not needed hypnosis to remember it. So, was it true? Had he dreamed it? Or had he made it up? But then other people started to report that they, too, had experienced similar alien encounters.

Here's how an artist showed the night that Brazilian "farmer" Antonio Villas Boas was abducted by alien visitors.

Alien Landings

First, there were reports of UFOs. Then, evidence that the aliens had landed began to appear.

The first report of so-called flying saucers was made in 1947 by Kenneth Arnold, a businessman from Idaho. He was flying his plane over the Cascade Mountains when he saw "a formation of very bright objects, flying very close to the mountaintops and traveling at tremendous speed." This was followed by two mysterious events that were later to become known as the Roswell Incident.

MYSTERIOUS WRECKAGE

On the morning of June 14, 1947, rancher "Mac" Brazel found wreckage that spread for 400 yards (364 m) across his land to the northwest of the town of Roswell, New Mexico. It was like thin metallic foil and was very tough. Brazel reported his find to the U.S. Army base at Roswell. On July 8, troops went to the site and collected the wreckage. Later the Army announced that the wreckage was the remains of a weather balloon.

Also on July 8, civil engineer Grady Barnett was in the desert of New Mexico. He thought he saw an aircraft that had crashed, so he went to look at the wreckage. To his amazement he

"To his amazement he found 'some sort of metallic, disk-shaped object.'"

GRADY BARNETT'S DISCOVERY

found "some sort of metallic, disk-shaped object." It was about 30 feet (9 m) across. Bodies were lying on the ground beside it. Barnett said they were "like humans. But they were not humans." Military police arrived and roped off the area. Barnett told friends about his discovery, but all the civilians were told it was their duty to their country to say nothing.

Nearly 50 years later, an Air Force investigation into the Roswell Incident claimed that the "space-craft" was, in fact, a special balloon designed to keep an eye on Soviet nuclear testing as part of the U.S. government's top secret operation—Project Mogul. But the dead aliens have still not been explained.

"Riding high, and without sound, there was a gigantic, cigar-shaped silvery ship."

GEORGE ADAMSKI

A VISITOR FROM VENUS

Over the next few years, many other UFO sightings were reported. But nothing more was known about the occupants. Then, George Adamski, a fast-food restaurant worker from California, reported an encounter. On November 20, 1952, he took a trip into the nearby desert with a party of friends. They wanted to see if they could spot a UFO. They ate a picnic lunch. Then, reported Adamski: "Riding high, and without sound, there was a gigantic, cigar-shaped silvery ship." He grabbed a camera and set off along a dirt road. Soon he noticed a man standing about 450 yards (410 m) away. Adamski went closer.

A drawing of George Adamski's meeting with the alien Orthon. The meeting was allegedly witnessed from a distance by Adamski's friends.

"The beauty of his form surpassed [went beyond] anything I had ever seen," Adamski wrote later. The figure was about 5 feet 6 inches (1.65 m) tall. He weighed about 135 lbs. (61 kg). He looked to be in his late 20s. He had long, blond hair. His eyes were "calm, gray-green." They narrowed at the corners. He was wearing a one-piece suit with a wide belt.

The being told Adamski that his name was Orthon and that he was from the planet Venus. He had come to Earth to try to stop the testing of atomic weapons. Orthon told Adamski that all alien beings in the universe looked similar to humans. He also said humans were being abducted by aliens.

Then Orthon went back aboard the spacecraft. It took off. Adamski later produced a number of photographs. He said he had taken them at the time. He also said that on other occasions he was allowed to travel in flying saucers. He claimed to have visited Venus, Mars, and the far side of the Moon.

Adamski wrote this story as a piece of fiction. Later it was rewritten as the truth. The new book was called *Flying Saucers Have Landed*. In time, space exploration showed what the far side of the Moon was like. It did not match Adamski's description.

WORDS OF WARNING

Adamski's book was published in 1954. Soon afterward, books by other people began to appear. Orfeo Angelucci published his book *Secret of the Saucers* in 1955. He said he had his first contact with aliens on May 24, 1952. He received a message from the "Space Brothers." They were aboard a UFO in a field near Los Angeles.

They warned him that humankind was in danger. They also told him that their flying saucers could travel at the speed of light. Angelucci wrote that in July 1952 he had met with another UFO. This was parked under a freeway. He went aboard and it took off. He was then told all about the Space Brothers. A beam of white light shone on him and he "knew the mystery of life." He was told that, in a previous life, he had also been a

Truman Bethurum's book (above) described his meeting with a female alien in 1952. Later, Bethurum saw her in a restaurant. She denied knowing him. Could this book have influenced Adamski's story?

Space Brother. Later Angelucci met with the aliens in several public places. He said that he had visited their planet and had met Jesus of Nazareth. Angelucci said that Jesus had told him: "This is the beginning of the New Age."

"... a message of love and understanding."

HOWARD MENGER

The aliens told Angelucci that humans must learn to cooperate. If not, a dreadful, frightening event would happen on Earth in 1986. Strangely, there was a major accident at the Soviet nuclear power plant at Chernobyl on April 26, 1986. Huge clouds of radioactive material drifted across the Northern Hemisphere. Northern Sweden was badly affected.

MESSAGE OF LOVE

Yet another book was *From Outer Space to You*. It was written by Howard Menger in 1959. Menger claimed to have seen his first flying saucer in 1932. Ten years later, while he was in the U.S. Army, Menger claimed to have had many meetings with "Space People" from Venus, Mars, and Saturn.

However, during the early 1960s, Menger changed his story. He said that he had been working for the CIA all along. They were using him in an experiment. They had wanted to test the public's reaction to UFO sightings. But in 1967, Menger said his original story was true. He said he wanted to tell people "what people don't want to hear: a message of love and understanding."

The First Abductions

Many people claim to have been abducted by aliens. Can they all be making it up?

One of the most extraordinary tales of abduction by aliens was told by Betty Andreasson. It was the night of January 25, 1967. The little town of South Ashburnham, Massachusetts, was wrapped in thick fog. Suddenly all the lights in the Andreasson family home flickered and went out. At the same time, a pink light appeared through the kitchen window. Betty's father looked into the backyard. He later made a signed statement: "These creatures that I saw were just like Halloween freaks. I thought they had put on a funny kind of headdress imitating a moon man. The one in front looked at me and I felt kind of queer. That's all I knew."

WALKING THROUGH DOORS

The family fell into a deep trance. But Betty stayed awake. She saw the aliens walk right through a closed door into the house. They were about 4 feet (1.2 m) tall. They had gray skin, and their eyes were almost catlike. They wore shiny, close-fitting uniforms.

Betty told her story under hypnosis in 1977. She said the aliens communicated with her by telepathy (mind reading). The leader's name

People who have been abducted by aliens have all given similar descriptions of their captors (opposite).

16

". . . their heads and eyes were large, and they had small, slitted mouths."

was Quazgaa. She gave him a Bible. He gave her a thin blue book in exchange. He asked her to follow him "so that she could help to change the world." She hesitated, but she went outside. An oval-shaped spacecraft was in the yard.

A FANTASTIC VOYAGE

Betty went aboard. There, she was given a thorough physical examination. Some of it was painful. But the aliens relieved the pain by placing their hands on her forehead. Then she was given a chair to sit on. Hoses were attached to her nose and mouth. A clear, airtight cover was put over her. Gray fluid flowed into it. It seemed that this fluid was to protect her while the spacecraft was in flight.

Some time after, the gray fluid drained away. Betty was taken down a dark tunnel, which led out into a strange landscape. Everything, even the air, glowed red. She and the aliens floated down a track between square buildings. She saw strange creatures climbing around on the buildings. They had eyes on stalks. A big pyramid stood at the end of the track. Bright, colorful crystals floated in the air, filling it with light.

Betty then heard a loud voice calling her name. It told her that she had been specially chosen. After that, the

While the rest of Betty Andreasson's family fell into a trance, Betty saw a group of small aliens walk right through the closed door into the house (above).

18

aliens took her back to the spaceship. She was told that "secrets" had been put in her memory—secrets that were to help humankind.

Betty's family was still in a trance when she arrived home. The aliens led them all to bed. Three hours and 40 minutes had passed.

This is a close-up picture of a crystal of sodium chloride under polarized light. Was this what Betty Andreasson saw?

The next morning Betty could remember little about her experience. The thin blue book had disappeared. She could not remember the secrets she had been given. Nearly 10 years later she told her story under hypnosis. An examination by a psychiatrist confirmed she was sane.

ABDUCTED MEN

Herbert Schirmer was a policeman. He worked in the town of Ashland, Nebraska. It was December 3, 1967. In the early hours of the morning he was on the outskirts of town. The lights of the patrol car showed an object on the road.

At first, Schirmer thought it was a broken-down truck. Then, he shined his lights full on it. He saw a craft shaped like a huge football. It stood on three legs. Red lights were blinking around it. The lights blinked faster and faster. The UFO took off and disappeared in the dark sky.

The policeman had to write up the log of his night's work. There were 20 minutes that he could not account for. He had a bad headache and weird buzzing sounds in his ears. He also had a red bruise nearly 3 inches (7.6 cm) wide down the back of his neck. Schirmer was clearly in a state of shock. "My father was an Air Force career man," he said later. "My background just wasn't the kind that let you believe in spaceships from other worlds." He was asked to undergo hypnosis. When he did, he told an extraordinary story about the missing 20 minutes.

INSIDE A UFO

Schirmer spoke of an unknown force that prevented him from drawing his gun or using his car radio. Strange beings had come out of the UFO. They had surrounded him. One had fired a green gas that came out of a "boxlike thing." It had covered the patrol car. A bright white light shone through the windshield and paralyzed him. The beings were about 4 feet (1.2 m) tall. They were muscular but wiry, with broad chests. Their heads were narrow, and their eyes were like the eyes of a cat. They were dressed in silver-gray coveralls. Some kind of weapon hung from belts around their waists.

Schirmer was ordered to get out of the car. He noticed that the beings could breathe in Earth's atmosphere. He was led

Herbert Schirmer was frozen by the bright light from a UFO (above). He was then taken aboard the craft.

This is one artist's idea of a typical alien. Most witnesses have described them as small beings with large heads, catlike eyes, and silvery coveralls.

up a ladder into the UFO. It was very cold inside. The room was some 25 by 20 feet (7.5 by 6 m). One of the aliens touched the back of his neck. It hurt. The aliens told Schirmer they had come to Ashland to get power for their craft from the local electricity lines. They had come from a nearby galaxy and had several bases on Earth.

Schirmer asked if they abducted people. The aliens said they did. They used them in experiments to study human growth and development. Schirmer did not ask any more because he didn't want to be kidnapped himself! The aliens told him they would visit him again, and he was taken back to his car.

After his experience, Schirmer could not concentrate on his work. As a result, he decided to resign from the police force.

Staff Sergeant Charles Moody, of the U.S. Air Force, had a similar encounter. On August 13, 1975, he was at his base at Alamogordo, New Mexico. He was working a late shift and decided to drive out to watch the night sky. Suddenly a disk-shaped UFO came down toward him. The car wouldn't start. He heard a high-pitched noise and saw shadowy figures. He felt numb all over. The next thing he saw was the UFO leaving. Over an hour had passed.

During the next two months, he began to remember what had happened. He had been aboard the spacecraft. There were beings about 4 feet 8 inches (1.3 m) tall. They had grayish skin, their heads and eyes were large, and they had small, slitted mouths.

Their leader wore a silver uniform. Moody was taken on a tour of the UFO. The beings said that they feared nuclear weapons and that radar confused their navigation systems. They said that alien contact with humans would increase.

FIVE-DAY DISAPPEARANCE

Nearly three months later, on November 5, 1975, Travis Walton was working with a woodcutting crew in a forest near Snowflake, Arizona.

It was quite dark by 6:00 P.M., so the crew was leaving in their truck. A UFO landed on the dirt road in front of them. It was about 20 feet (6 m) wide and some 8 feet (2.4 m) high. It had a domed top and glowed gently with a "milky yellow" light.

When Travis Walton found himself aboard a UFO with three aliens, his first thought was to defend himself.

Walton walked toward the UFO. A beam of blue-green light shone from it. Suddenly he was thrown into the air. The truck driver was terrified and drove away. Walton was left alone with the UFO. Later, when the truck driver came back, Walton had vanished and the UFO had gone.

"This young man is not lying. He really believes these things."

DR. GENE ROSENBAUM

Walton was missing for five days. Then, he phoned his sister from Heber—a town 12 miles (19 km) away. He said he had woken up in a room aboard the UFO. There were three aliens in the room. They were about 5 feet (1.5 m) tall; they were thin; and they had large, bald heads and huge black eyes. He went to attack them, and they left the room. He ran after them. He found himself in what he thought was the control room.

A figure wearing a helmet led Walton away from the control room. The figure seemed to be human. Walton also saw other humans. A mask was put over his face, and he lost consciousness. When he awoke, he was on the ground. The UFO was soaring into the sky above him.

Later, Walton took a polygraph test. The test uses electrical brainwaves to help determine if someone is telling the truth. Dr. Gene Rosenbaum carried out the test. He stated, "This young man is not lying. He really believes these things."

Aliens Worldwide

In the 1960s and 1970s, people in South America and Europe were visited by aliens.

There are many lavender farms in Provence, France (opposite). One day in 1965, Maurice Masse found a UFO standing in one of his fields.

The first reports of aliens were mainly in the United States. Then sightings in South America and Europe began to be reported.

Iñácio da Souza was a hired hand on a ranch at Pilar de Goiás, Brazil. On August 13, 1967, he and his wife spotted three figures standing on the landing strip of the ranch. They were wearing unusual, yellow, skintight clothes. When they saw the da Souza couple, the figures came toward them. Then, Iñácio saw a strange craft on the runway. It was "like an upturned washbasin." He became frightened and fired the gun he was carrying. A beam of green light shone from the UFO. It struck his head and shoulders. The three figures ran to the craft. It took off. The next day, Iñácio became seriously ill. No one will ever know if there was a connection between the green light and his illness. Iñácio died within two months.

ALIEN COMMUNICATIONS

On January 21, 1976, Herminio Reis was driving with his wife, Bianca. They were on the highway that runs from Rio de Janeiro to Belo Horizonte, Brazil. At about 11:30 P.M., they

24

"Reports of alien visitors also began to come from all over Europe."

stopped for a rest. Herminio fell asleep. He was awakened by Bianca's scream. All around them, they reported later, was a brilliant blue light. The car was "absorbed—as if through a chimney." They found themselves in a circular area that was brightly lit.

"They said that they had overcome old age. There was no death in their world."

Two tall, strange-looking beings came up to the car. They made signs for the couple to get out. When they spoke, it was in a language that Herminio and Bianca could not understand. The couple was led up a staircase into a room. Each was given a headset, and one of the beings also put a headset on its head. This was plugged into what looked like a computer. Through their headsets, the Reis's heard a voice. It spoke in Portuguese, the language of Brazil. It said, "My name is Karen. Calm down."

EVERLASTING LIFE

Bianca had her skin, ears, and eyes examined by the aliens. Then she was placed in a type of box that glowed red-hot like a grill. She felt something like an electric shock, and then lost consciousness. When she awoke, she was lying on a table that was exactly the shape of her body. More beings appeared. One was a tall, dark-haired woman. The couple was told that the aliens were carrying out medical research. They said that they had overcome old age. There was no death in their world.

26

Bianca was given an instrument for communication. Then the couple were returned to their car. They found themselves back on the highway. Bianca later said she was still communicating with Karen.

VISITORS TO EUROPE

Reports of alien visitors also began to come from all over Europe. One of the first was from Italy. In November 1954, Signora Rosa Lotti-Danielli was on her way to a cemetery in the town of Arezzo. She was carrying a bunch of flowers. Suddenly she saw a UFO. Two beings appeared. Each was about 4 feet (1.2 m) tall. They spoke to her in a language she could not understand. One took the flowers. Signora Lotti-Danielli ran away and called the police. When she returned with them, the UFO had gone. But other people said they had seen it leave.

This illustration appeared in an Italian magazine in 1954. It accompanied the story of Rosa Lotti-Danielli's encounter with aliens while on her way to Arezzo.

Maurice Masse grew lavender (fragrant lilac-purple flowers) in fields near Valensole, which is in Provence, France. It was soon after dawn on July 1, 1965. Masse was on his way to work in the fields when he heard a whistling sound. He thought it must be a helicopter. Then, Masse saw a UFO among the lavender bushes about 100 yards (91 m) away.

It was shaped like a football with a dome on top. It stood on six legs. It looked, said Masse, "like an enormous spider." Two small figures were near the craft. They were examining the lavender bushes. Masse thought they were young boys. However, when he got closer to them, he saw they were not human. They were about 3 feet (90 cm) tall. Their skin was white, and their heads were huge. But they had no chins, and their mouths were just round holes. Their ears were large, and their big, catlike eyes had no lids. They wore one-piece suits, colored gray-green. Masse noticed that they had no hair.

SCORCHED EARTH

Masse started creeping up on the aliens. One noticed him and took a small cylinder from its belt. The alien pointed it at Masse, who found he could not move. The aliens stared at him. They spoke to each other in grunts; then they went back to their spacecraft. They entered it through a sliding door, and the whistling noise began again. Then, the UFO took off quickly and disappeared.

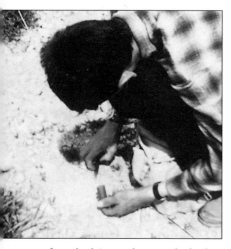

A geologist examines marks in the ground at the site where Maurice Masse claimed to have seen a UFO.

There was evidence for Masse's story. Something had definitely been in the lavender fields. A strip of plants that was 300 feet (90 m) long and about 10 feet (3 m) wide had been damaged by heat. Also, there were strange marks in the earth where Masse saw the UFO standing.

Later revealed to be a hoax, this "photograph" of a flying saucer was taken in Switzerland in 1975 by Eduard Meier.

TOO GOOD TO BE TRUE?

On the afternoon of January 28, 1975, Swiss farmer Eduard "Billy" Meier was out walking near his home in the region of Zurich. He saw a large silver disk in the sky. It was about 25 feet (7.5 m) wide. He had his camera with him, so he took a series of photographs. Then, the UFO landed about 100 yards (91 m) away from Meier. He ran toward it, but some kind of force stopped him from reaching it. A figure came out of the disk and approached him.

Meier said that he communicated with the alien for nearly two hours. The visitor said he came from the Pleiades, a star group some 430 light-years away from Earth. Over the next three years, Meier claimed to have had 105 meetings with other aliens. He said he had taken over 500 photographs and written 3,000 pages of notes. Meier's photographs were good and clear. Later they underwent a computer test. The verdict was that they were all hoaxes.

Strange Creatures

Terrifying "monsters" lurk at the back of everyone's imagination. Many such monsters have been brought to life in Hollywood films like *Gremlins* and *Men in Black*. But do such unearthly creatures really exist?

It was the night of August 21, 1955. Billy Ray Taylor and his wife and children were visiting Elmer Sutton and his family at their farm near Hopkinsville, Kentucky. Billy went to the well in the yard to draw water. Suddenly he saw something land in the gulch nearby. It was very big. Billy Ray said it was "real bright; but with an exhaust all the colors of the rainbow."

A SCARY ORDEAL

An hour later a dog began barking in the yard. Elmer and Billy Ray thought there might be an intruder. They grabbed their guns and opened the door. A tiny, "shining," figure approached them. Elmer and Billy Ray fired at it. The bullets hit the figure, making a strange sound. It was "as if you had shot into a pail."

The figure was thrown backward, then it fled. But more creatures arrived. They were a little over 3 feet (90 cm) high. Their heads were

Many Hollywood movies create terrifying creatures (opposite) to play on people's fear of monsters. But do such alien beings really exist?

30

**". . . can such unearthly
creatures really exist?"**

The magazine Thrilling Wonder Stories *(above), produced in the 1930s, told tales of many weird and terrifying aliens.*

egg-shaped, and their eyes were large and yellow. They also had huge, flappy ears like an elephant's. Their arms were long and thin, with claws on the end, where hands would normally be. Their bodies were silvery and seemed to be lit from inside.

A creature climbed onto the roof. Elmer and Billy Ray both fired at it. It floated some 40 feet (12 m), then landed on a fence. They fired again. It fell from the fence and disappeared on all fours into the weeds. However, the creatures were not killed by the shots. Instead, their lighted bodies just got brighter. They seemed more frightened by the light from flashlights.

CURIOUS CREATURES

The families were terrified and locked themselves inside the house. The creatures waited outside for three hours. They peeped in through the windows. Then, the families ran for their cars and drove to Hopkinsville, where they alerted the police.

Six police officers searched the farm but found nothing. They left at about 2:00 A.M. The families went to bed. However, the creatures returned. Again they surrounded the house, but they made no move against the families. They finally left at 5:15 A.M.

MIND GAMES

John Hodges had an even more terrifying encounter when alien visitors of a very different kind appeared in south Los Angeles, almost 16 years later.

In August 1971, Hodges and Peter Rodriguez had been visiting a friend in Dapple Gray Lane. At about 2:00 A.M., they left in Hodges's car to return home. In the roadway they saw two objects. These looked like human "brains." Each was almost 3 feet (90 cm) high, and they appeared to be alive! Hodges quickly drove around them. He took Rodriguez home, then drove to his own apartment. But he arrived there two hours later than he expected.

AN ALIEN EXPERIMENT

Many years later, Hodges underwent hypnosis. He recalled that on that night in 1971 the "brains" were

Not all aliens have a human-like form, as John Hodges found out in 1971. Some are more monstrous. This model is the head of "Lam," a creature that supposedly came to Earth in 1919.

waiting outside his apartment. They seemed to project him from his car into a room filled with strange machines. There, aliens warned him of the dangers of nuclear war. They said that Hodges would see them again. This happened in 1978.

Hodges was told he had an implant in his brain to heighten his psychic awareness. The aliens said that this had also been done to others. They also said the human race was just the result of biological experiments that they had carried out over millions of years.

Recent Experiences

Most reports of aliens come from the 1950s and 1960s. However, encounters are still being reported to this day.

In November 1987, Ed Walters encountered a UFO outside his home (opposite). It was the first of many sightings by Walters.

Alfred Burtoo, an Englishman in his late 70s, had a strange experience on August 12, 1983. He was fishing near an Army base in Aldershot, Hampshire, when he heard a clock striking 1:00 A.M. He saw a very bright light descending and thought that it was an Army helicopter. Then, two beings came up to him. Burtoo said they were about 4 feet 6 inches (1.35 m) tall. Each wore green overalls and a mask over its face. They made signs that he was to follow them.

TOO OLD FOR ALIENS

The aliens took Burtoo to a circular UFO. Burtoo went inside, and one of the beings spoke to him. Burtoo was asked his age, and he was told to stand under an amber light. Some minutes passed. Then one of the beings told him: "You can go. You are too old and infirm for our purpose." He left the UFO. It flew off at great speed. A whole hour had passed.

Budd Hopkins was an American artist and author. He was interested in such tales. During the 1980s, he began to investigate them. He questioned many people under hypnosis. One was Linda Cortile, of Manhattan.

"He wanted to take more pictures, but he was hit by a beam of blue light."

On August 12, 1983, 77-year-old Alfred Burtoo had a narrow escape. He was abducted by aliens in Aldershot, England (above). But the aliens told him he was "too old . . . for our purpose."

UNUSUAL ABDUCTION

In April 1989, Mrs. Cortile contacted Budd Hopkins. She told him she had been abducted by aliens. It had happened about 20 years earlier.

On November 30, 1989, she contacted Hopkins again. She said she had been abducted again! It had happened in the early hours of that morning. She had seen a gray being come into her bedroom. She could not wake her husband, so she threw a pillow at the being. Then she found she was unable to move. Her mind went blank. Under hypnosis, Linda recalled the night's events.

Three or four aliens had entered the room. She was "floated" out through the closed window. It was 12 stories above the street. There was a beam of blue light. It came from a UFO. The UFO was hovering above the apartment building. Mrs. Cortile was taken aboard. A medical examination was carried out on her. Then she was returned to her bed.

In itself, this account was not unusual. It is identical to many others. However, what happened later made it seem very strange. In February 1991, Budd Hopkins received a letter. It was signed only "Dan" and "Richard." The writers said they were police officers. They had seen Mrs. Cortile's abduction.

WITNESSES IN HIGH PLACES

In the letter, Richard and Dan described how Linda had floated gracefully into the UFO. Then the craft had flown off. It had entered the water of the East River, near the Brooklyn Bridge in New York City, and disappeared. The letter went on to say that the writers had waited 45 minutes. They did not see the UFO emerge. They were concerned about Linda's safety.

This photograph of Linda Cortile was taken at a UFO conference in 1993.

Some weeks after the arrival of the letter, Linda called Hopkins. She told him the officers had visited her. They were relieved to find her safe. They said that they could not meet Hopkins, but that they would contact him again. Soon he received more information. It included a tape-recorded message. This message was supposedly from one of the officers.

The voice on the tape spoke about Dan and Richard. It said that they were two Secret Service agents. On the night of November 30, 1989, they had been on duty. They were taking Perez de

Cuellar—a Peruvian diplomat and Secretary General of the United Nations (U.N.)—to a heliport. Their car had suddenly broken down, so they had pushed it into a nearby parking space. This was close to Mrs. Cortile's apartment. The voice on the tape went on to say that Perez de Cuellar had also seen the abduction, and the UFO.

"CASE OF THE CENTURY"

Shortly after this, Linda made another claim. She said she had been bundled into a car by Richard and Dan. They asked her if she was an alien. They made her take off her shoes. This was to prove she had toes. Aliens, they said, did not. Linda made a note of the license plate of the car. She also noted the number of another car that seemed to be tailing the first one. It turned out that the numbers belonged to the British and Venezuelan missions to the U.N. Hopkins believed this to be "the case of the century." But it seems that he was the victim of a hoax. Officials at the U.N. were contacted and asked about the Perez de Cuellar connection. They checked out the details of the night in question. But they said de Cuellar had not been on his way to the heliport. He was at home in bed!

After her encounter with aliens in 1989, Linda Cortile's abduction was drawn by an artist.

38

A VOICE IN THE HEAD

Budd Hopkins had also written about the strange story of another alien encounter.

Budd Hopkins—artist and author specializing in alien abductions.

This had happened in Gulf Breeze, an area of Florida near Pensacola. It was the late afternoon of November 11, 1987. Ed Walters saw a UFO moving behind some trees across the street from his home. He picked up his camera and took several pictures; then he ran outside. He wanted to take more pictures, but he was hit by a beam of blue light. He could not move. He felt himself lifted up. A voice in his head said, "We will not harm you." He resisted. His mind was filled with images of dogs. Then, the light and the UFO disappeared. Walters fell to the ground.

The photographs that Walters had taken were developed and published in the local newspaper. The former editor of the paper, Charles Somerby, said he and his wife had also seen the UFO. So had a local resident, Mrs. Zammit.

Ed Walters saw the same UFO many times over the next six months. He took more photographs. UFO investigators helped him. They gave him a special sealed camera. This, too, produced photographs of a spacecraft. It was about 12 feet (3.6 m) across, and 9 feet (2.7 m) wide. It seemed to have some type of bright "power ring" below it. Walters always knew when the UFO was going to appear. He would hear a strange buzzing noise inside his head. It was suggested that this was caused by a device that had been put in his head during his first encounter.

"A white light shone from the craft. . . . Aliens emerged and came toward him."

On December 2, 1987, Walters saw an alien being in his backyard. He chased it away. On January 12, 1988, he was in his pickup. He saw the UFO and photographed it. A white light shone from the craft. It paralyzed him. Aliens emerged and came toward him. But he managed to drive away.

Things reached a climax on May 1. Walters took his 39th picture of the UFO. Then he blacked out. He eventually revived, but an hour and a quarter had passed. He believed that he had been taken aboard the craft, where the device in his head was removed.

These experiences were reported nationwide. But there were doubts. Someone said they had discovered a model UFO in the loft of Walters's home. It looked very like the one in his photos. Then a young man offered an explanation. He said that he had helped Walters to fake the photographs. However, Walters passed a polygraph test. The debate about the Walters' photos continues.

TRAGIC CONSEQUENCES

The interest in alien visitors to Earth remains strong. In recent years, however, this interest has led to a number of human tragedies.

40

The Hale-Bopp comet, with its long, trailing "tail," could be seen clearly by the naked eye. It was only 125 million miles (201 million km) away from Earth when it passed by in March 1997.

In March 1997, 39 people gathered at Rancho Santa Fe, San Diego, California. Each one was dressed in identical clothes—white shirts and black pants. The gathering of people had been triggered by the appearance of the Hale-Bopp comet, which, at that time, could be seen in orbit around the Earth.

The people were led by two men, Father Logan and Father Jean, who had claimed to be aliens. Their belief regarding the comet was highly unusual. They told their followers that the comet was being trailed by a spacecraft. They hoped they would be taken aboard the craft and carried off to heaven. Believing this, the followers were encouraged to die. But there was no such heaven-bound spacecraft.

What Is the Truth?

These have been just some of the many stories about aliens. But should we believe them?

Most accounts of alien visitors and abductions are similar, but this does not make them more likely to be true. Stories of UFOs have been circulating for 50 years. People could, therefore, make up new stories, using details from the old ones to make them more believable.

Many people who say they have been taken aboard a UFO have to be hypnotized before they can remember anything. They are encouraged to relive the experience. What happens then depends on the hypnotist. It is difficult for the hypnotist to avoid making suggestions. And some questions will produce certain answers. The hypnotist may ask: "Are the eyes catlike?" Or "Are they green?" Most people under hypnosis are eager to please. They may not actually remember. So they are likely to answer, yes.

THE BOUNDARIES OF SPACE

This 1927 cover from the science-fiction magazine Amazing Stories *(opposite) illustrates one of the events in H. G. Wells's classic story,* War of the Worlds.

In the early days, aliens were said to come from the Moon. Sometimes they were from Venus or Mars. Then, space probes ventured farther into the galaxy and proved that this was not possible. Later, aliens were said to come from unknown planets in far-distant star systems.

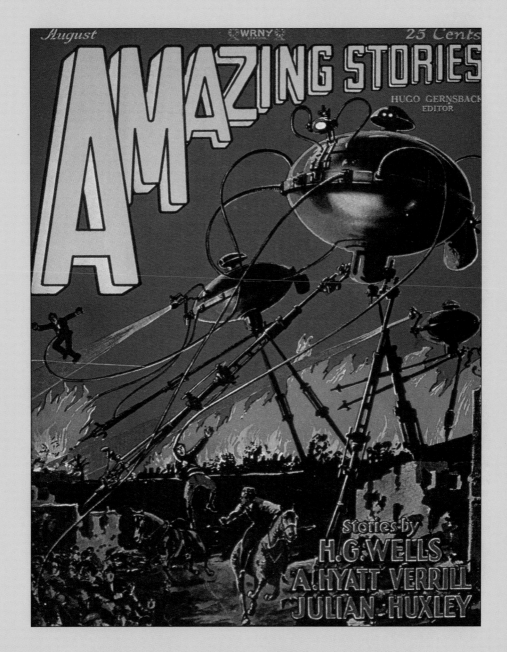

"... things are different in science fiction. Spaceships travel immense distances...."

The landing probe from Viking 2 *took this photograph on the surface of Mars in the mid-1970s. Scientists decided that aliens could not come from this planet.*

For decades, astronomers were sure aliens could not exist. Recently, however, distant planets have been discovered, and some may support life. In 1997 astronomers made a big discovery. They thought there might be life on one of Jupiter's moons. But there are no reports of alien visitors being from there.

FACT AND FICTION

If aliens do exist, they are now thought to come from planets hundreds of light-years away. A light-year is the distance a beam of light can travel in one year. That is about 6 trillion miles! Scientists keep trying to find ways of making space travel faster, but they believe that it is impossible to ever reach a speed that comes close to the speed of light.

However, things are different in science fiction. Spaceships are able to travel immense distances by entering "hyperspace," which is an entirely imaginary part of space in which it is possible to travel faster than the speed of light. But this is pure fiction.

Science-fiction magazines became popular in the U.S. in the 1920s. Two of the best known were *Weird Tales* and *Amazing Stories*. They told tales of "strange adventures on other worlds." People met alien races. Often the aliens were similar to humans. But their heads were much bigger, and their skin was a different color. They looked like "little green men from Mars." Many people became familiar with that phrase. So where did the idea come from?

A MODERN MYTH

The psychologist Carl Jung, who practiced in Vienna, Austria, at the same time as Sigmund Freud, had an interesting theory. He noticed that people all over the world told the same kind of folktales. These people had never met, nor even heard about, one another. Yet every culture has similar stories about monsters, dragons, serpents, giants, and mysterious, unexplained events. We call these stories myths.

"They looked like 'little green men from Mars.' "

TYPICAL SCIENCE-FICTION DESCRIPTION OF ALIENS

Jung had a theory for the sources of these myths. He believed they were part of basic human personality and developed with the human brain. It was similar to how social behavior developed. So myths are deep in the subconscious of every human being. The myths gradually took on traditional forms and were then passed on. One generation passed them on to the next. Jung said the same was true of the UFO. It was developing as a modern myth.

LITTLE GREEN MEN

On September 23, 1880, David Lang mysteriously disappeared from a field at Gallatin, Tennessee. One second he was in full view of his wife and two children, his brother-in-law, and Judge August Peck. The next second he had vanished. In June 1900, Sherman Church ran into a cotton mill near Lake Michigan. He was never seen again. There have been many such mysterious disappearances over the years. In the old days, people would have said they had been "stolen by the little people."

Do you believe in "little people?" Today, most of us would answer, "No!" But for centuries, people did believe in their existence. They were called goblins in Germany; pixies in Scotland; leprechauns in Ireland. All these "little people" were extremely small. Often their skin and their clothes were green. They could fly through the air, and they could vanish at will. Many folktales feature unfortunate people who met "little people" by night, or who saw a group feasting and dancing. As a result, they were carried off to never-never land. Sometimes they came back. If they did, they discovered that time had mysteriously passed.

All these stories sound very much like the stories of alien abductions. It looks as if Carl Jung might have been right. Alien abductions could be the biggest 20th century myth.

Toy leprechauns at an Irish fair in Los Angeles. Could such mythical beings be the basis for tales of 20th century alien abductions?

Glossary

abducted Kidnapped, or removed from a place, usually by force.

abduction Another name for a kidnapping. "It was an abduction."

encounters Sudden, unexpected meetings with a person or thing.

freeway An expressway, or toll-free highway.

galaxy A group of stars and planets. There are billions of galaxies in the universe.

geologist A scientist who studies the history of Earth's structure.

gulch A narrow, stony valley caused by the rushing of a stream before it dried up.

hypnosis A sleeplike state in which a person is totally relaxed. In this state, the person's mind can be "opened" to remember otherwise forgotten events.

hypnotist A person who is able to put another person into a sleeplike state of hypnosis.

implant Something that is fixed deeply in the body or mind. Can be an object or an idea.

impression An image of something, or an idea, that is produced from the imagination.

investigation A thorough examination of a person or thing.

nuclear Of or concerning nuclear energy or weapons. Nuclear energy is the powerful force produced when the central part, or nucleus, of an atom is split or joined to another atom.

ordeal A difficult or painful experience.

psychiatrist A person who treats those with mental disabilities.

psychic awareness Powers of the mind that cannot be scientifically explained.

psychologist A person who studies the human mind and human behavior.

radioactive Something that gives off harmful energy in the form of radiation, such as a nuclear bomb.

surpassed Went beyond expected achievements, or a result that was better than hoped for.

telepathy Mind reading, or the sending of thoughts from one person's mind to another.

theory A reasonable idea that has not been proved.

trance A sleeplike condition of the mind while a person is awake.

UFO Any unidentified flying object in the skies.

verdict A judgment or decision.

47

Index

Further Reading

Asimov, Isaac, et al. *UFOs: True Mysteries or Hoaxes.* Gareth Stevens, 1995
Deary, Terry. *Alien Landings.* Larousse Kingfisher Chambers, 1996
Kettelkamp, Larry. *ETs & UFOs: Are They for Real?* Morrow, 1996
Klass, Philip J. *Bringing UFOs Down to Earth.* Prometheus Books, 1997
Landau, Elaine. *UFOs,* "Mysteries of Science" series. Millbrook Press, 1995